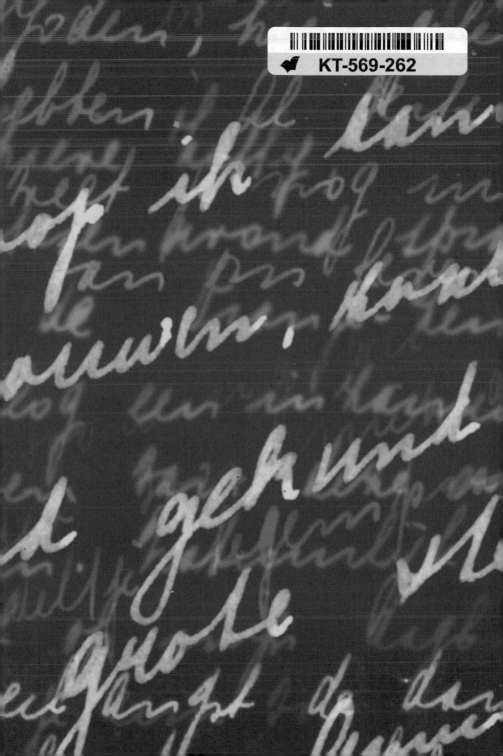

a History
for Today
Anne Frank

ANNE FRANK HOUSE

Contents

Preface

Since its first publication in 1947, millions of people around the world have read the diary of Anne Frank, giving a succession of new generations a penetrating look at the persecution of the Jews during World War Two. What was it like to be a Jewish child hiding in the Netherlands during the Nazi occupation? What was it like to go through every minute of the day afraid of being discovered, and wondering what would happen afterwards? Anne Frank, her family and a few of their friends spent more than two years hidden in the Secret Annex. A few of her father's employees helped them, thereby risking their own lives.

In her diary, Anne is able to describe her own development as well as the major and minor events that took place during their years in hiding. The threatening outside world is never absent from the book's pages. She writes not only about her fears but also about her hopes and expectations. Anne Frank became a victim of the persecution of the Jews. In confronting her life story we are made acutely aware that the persecution of the Jews did not annihilate an *anonymous* six million. The Holocaust was the genocide of the Jewish people: it was the murder six million times over of unique individuals, of human beings.

National Socialism suffered a military defeat in 1945, but the body of thought that gave rise to National Socialism continues to haunt the world today in a variety of forms. Anti-Semitism and racism have not been eradicated. There are still those who think that some people are more valuable than others, that their own people are superior to other groups. In the 1990s, the concept of "racial purity" reappeared in the Balkans with the horrifying practice of "ethnic cleansing."

The goal of the Anne Frank House is to keep alive the memory of Anne Frank and the period when National Socialism was in power. This is not only a matter of human and historical interest; it also has significance for us today. For the Anne Frank House, the memory of Anne Frank is directly related to a concern for preserving freedom and maintaining human rights and a pluralistic and democratic society. Through its activities, it attempts to inspire people all over the world to become actively involved in this effort.

Hans Westra
Director of the Anne Frank House

"Writing in a diary is a really strange experience for someone like me. Not only because I've never written anything before, but also because it seems to me that later on neither I nor anyone else will be interested in the musings of a thirteen-year-old schoolgirl."
  (Anne Frank)

On her thirteenth birthday, Anne Frank is given a diary. She has no way of knowing that in only a few weeks her life will undergo a complete change, and that for more than two years she will use her diary to record all her thoughts, feelings and experiences. Neither can she foresee that later on her diary will be read by millions of people all around the world.

"One single Anne Frank moves us more than the countless others who suffered just as she did, but whose faces have remained in the shadows. Perhaps it is better that way: if we were capable of taking in the suffering of all those people, we would not be able to live."
(Primo Levi)

"I wonder, must a person become a martyr, published posthumously, in order to be accepted and respected by those who live on her block?"
(Irene Frisch)

"Of the multitude who throughout history have spoken for human dignity in times of great suffering and loss, no voice is more compelling than that of Anne Frank."
(John F. Kennedy)

"The content of Anne Frank's legacy is still very much alive and it can address us fully, especially at a time when the map of the world is changing and when dark passions are awakening within people."
(Vaclav Havel)

"The diary is the spontaneous utterance of a young person, a girl who, despite the oppressiveness and anxiety that came with living underground, tried to grow and to free herself from her parents, searching for her own way."
(Laureen Nussbaum)

"The diary demonstrates the immense tragedy of the Holocaust, the waste of human lives and talent, and the price that was paid because free people did not act in time to oppress totalitarian movements."
(Yehuda Lev)

"Some of us read Anne Frank's diary on Robben Island and derived much encouragement of it."
(Nelson Mandela)

"I was born on June 12, 1929"

"My father, the most adorable father I've ever seen, didn't marry my mother until he was thirty-six and she was twenty-five. My sister Margot was born in Frankfurt am Main in Germany in 1926. I was born on June 12, 1929."

(ANNE FRANK)

1929

Anne Frank is the second daughter of Otto Frank and Edith Frank-Holländer. The Frank and Holländer families have lived in Germany for generations. The Franks are a liberal Jewish family. They feel a connection with the Jewish religion, but they are not strictly observant.

Anne's father and her Uncle Robert fought for Germany during World War One (1914-1918). Anne's grandmother, Alice Frank-Stern, volunteered at a military hospital during that war.

1 Anne and her mother.
2 Neighborhood children admiring baby Anne.
3 Frankfurt am Main, 1919.
4 Anne's father (left) and her Uncle Robert as German officers.
5 The wedding of Anne's parents on May 12, 1925.
6 Anne's grandmother as a nurse during the First World War.

World War One ends in 1918 with Germany's defeat. Heavy reparations are imposed on Germany under the terms of the Treaty of Versailles. Millions of people lose their jobs and are reduced to desperate poverty. Inflation soars; by 1923 the currency is practically worthless. Many Germans become embittered and harbor feelings of revenge. A small political party of extreme nationalists under the leadership of Adolf Hitler claims to have the solution to all these problems.

1929

9

10

7   Collecting money for needy
    children in Berlin, 1920.
8   Hitler in Nuremberg, 1927.
9   Sky-high inflation: by 1923
    the currency has lost almost
    all its value.
10 A demonstration at the
    Reichstag Berlin protesting
    the Treaty of Versailles.
11 The synagogue on the
    Börneplatz and the Weekly
    Market in Frankfurt am
    Main, 1927. In 1930, 1 percent
    of the German population
    - around 500,000 people -
    are Jewish.

11

"Anne in a rain puddle, crowing with pleasure"

"One morning I discovered Anne on the balcony in the rain, standing in the middle of a puddle and crowing with pleasure. She didn't move a muscle when I scolded her. She just wanted me to tell her a story, right away."

(KATI STILGENBAUER)

1929 – 1932

Kati is Anne's baby sitter. Anne loves stories, and she often plays with her sister and the other neighborhood children, many of whom have different religious and social backgrounds.

The acute economic crisis of October 1929 hits many people in Germany very hard. Business declines at the bank where Anne and Margot's father works, but compared to many other people the Frank family are managing quite well.

1 Anne and Margot with neighborhood children.
2 "Hitler: our last hope." NSDAP election poster from 1932.
3 Unemployed people lining up outside the employment bureau in Hannover. The words on the fence read: "Vote for Hitler."
4 Anne, Margot and their father, 1930.
5 Anne and her mother, 1931.
6 Margot's first day of school. Like other children, she is given a "Zuckertüte" (candy treat) on this day.

As the Depression grows in severity, more and more Germans are drawn to radical, anti-democratic parties. Both the Communists and the National Socialists claim to have *the* solution for every problem. Increasingly, political differences are fought out in the streets. The battle is won by the NSDAP, and in the 1932 election the party becomes the largest in parliament with 37 percent of the vote.

8

7

1929 · 1932

7 A demonstration against the NSDAP in 1932.
8 Berlin, 1932. The text on the wall reads: "Our children are wasting away here."
9 Supporters of Hitler march through Nuremberg during the "Reichsparteitag" of 1929.
10 Hitler with his admirers in 1932.

11 The NSDAP is one of the many splinter parties that emerge during the 1920s. After the 1932 elections the NSDAP is the country's largest party.

KPD: Kommunistische Partei Deutschlands
SPD: Sozialdemokratische Partei Deutschlands
ZP: Zentrumpartei
DNVP: Deutschnationale Volkspartei
NSDAP: National-sozialistishe Deutsche Arbeiterpartei

KPD
SPD
ZP
DNVP
NSDAP

1924
1928
1932

"The world around me collapsed"

"The world around me collapsed.... I had to face the consequences, and though this did hurt me deeply I realized that Germany was not the world and I left forever."

(OTTO FRANK)

1933

1 Edith, Anne and Margot
in Frankfurt am Main on
March 10, 1933, two days
before the municipal
elections. The elections
are won by the NSDAP.
2 Adolf Hitler becomes
Chancellor on January 30,
1933.
3 NSDAP torchlight proces-
sion through Berlin, 1933.
4 Arrested Communists,
March 6, 1933.
5 Photo booth picture of
Anne Frank, made at Tietz
Department Store.

On January 30, 1933, Hitler becomes
Chancellor of Germany. The new rulers soon
reveal their true intentions. The first anti-
Jewish measures are taken and a witch hunt
is launched against the Jews of Germany.

For Otto Frank the time to leave Germany
has come. He tries to find work in the
Netherlands where he has some business
contacts. His attempt succeeds. The Frank
family emigrates to Amsterdam.

The NSDAP takes action not only against the Jews but also against the party's political opponents. Communists and Social Democrats in particular are targeted and imprisoned in concentration camps. Certain genres of art, literature and music are also forbidden. Books are burned in the streets. Many writers, artists and scientists flee the country. Democracy is abolished. Only **one** truth prevails.

1933

6 On March 5th 1933, the SS comes to the assistance of the Berlin police.

7 On March 23, 1933, Parliament votes that Hitler can rule without its consent. The Social Democrats - those who have not yet been arrested or fled the country - provide the only opposing votes. The Communist Party has already been outlawed. The democratic Weimar Republic has turned into an NSDAP dictatorship.

8

8 The foreign media provide extensive coverage of the Nazi reign of terror. But this does not stop the National Socialists from organizing a boycott of all Jewish lawyers, doctors and shops on April 1, 1933.

9

10

9 A public book-burning is held in May 1933. The authors, many of whom are Jewish, are labeled "un-German."

10 "Führer, we follow you! Everyone says Yes!" By mid-1933, all political parties have been prohibited. The only party permitted to exist is the NSDAP.

"It was so nationalistic..."

Otto Treumann

"Even as a Jewish boy of fourteen I was somewhat
fascinated by everything that was going on. The
media were completely in thrall to the Nazi party. It
took hold of you, whether you liked it or not. It was so
nationalistic ... feeling 'German' and identifying with
the fatherland were extremely appealing, now that the
country was scrambling to its feet after the defeat of
1918. Scary? Absolutely! Especially when you knew
that you were Jewish and that all the problems were
being blamed on you. It was an inescapable,
inevitable and deadly threat!"

Nationalism then
The Nazis provided millions of people with
new security and hope for a better future.
They stimulated nationalistic feelings, and
with enormous success: it was the "we"
feeling of being German in the face of a
hostile world. The Jews were blamed for
everything and were branded as the German
people's greatest enemy.

1   Otto Treumann,
    around 1934.
2   Otto Treumann

Nationalism now

More than 50 years have passed since the
war ended, and prejudice, intolerance,
discrimination and racism have not
disappeared. Many people are strongly
attracted to extreme nationalism. The
powerful "we" feeling and exaggerated self-
esteem give many a sense of security.
Scapegoats are sought for present-day
problems within national borders and
beyond. Minorities are often the target.

"We emigrated to Holland"

"Because we're Jewish, my father emigrated to Holland in 1933, when he became the Managing Director of the Dutch Opekta Company, which manufactures products used in making jam."

(ANNE FRANK)

1935

1934

Otto Frank starts setting up his business: the sale of pectin for preparing homemade jam. The Frank family moves into a row house that is part of a new housing complex on the Merwedeplein in Amsterdam. Their neighborhood soon fills up with refugees from Germany. Anne and Margot are enrolled in school and quickly learn Dutch.

1 Anne at the Montessori School, 1935.
2 Otto Frank and his Austrian secretary Miep Santrouschitz. Miep came to the Netherlands in 1919.
3 The house on the Merwedeplein in Amsterdam where the Frank family lived.
4 The Frank family often goes to the beach.
5 Anne with her friend Sanne on the Merwedeplein.
6 Anne occasionally visits Grandma Holländer in Bad Aachen, Germany.

7

"Law and order" finally return to Germany. Prosperity is on the upswing. One of the Nazis' highest priorities is the training of young people. The enthusiasm for Hitler and his party is enormous. There are some opponents, but most of them remain silent, fearful of violence and imprisonment. The anti-Jewish measures are simply endured: few people resist them.

1934 – 1935

8

9

nd dient dem Führer

LLE ZEHNJÄHRIGEN IN DIE H.J.

10

7   On the beach in Germany.
8   The years 1934 and 1935 are marked by economic recovery. Unemployment declines sharply: jobless people are put to work constructing highways and government buildings and in the public sector. Hitler also begins building an arms industry and amassing a huge army.
9   "Young people serve the Leader." "All ten-year-olds in the Hitlerjugend (H.J. - Hitler Youth)."
10 Rigidly organized mass rallies make a big impression.
11 The Nazis want total control in the raising of Germany's young people. Boys' activities take on an increasingly militaristic tone. Girls are prepared for motherhood and home-making.

11

"If they saw us together..."

"If they saw us together now they'd arrest us." This is Otto Frank's comment to Gertrud Naumann, a non-Jewish friend of the family, while walking with her during his last trip to Germany in 1937.

1

2

1935 1937

In 1935, a series of "racial laws" is enacted in Germany stipulating that only those with "German blood" can be full-fledged citizens. The rights of everyone else are curtailed. Many regulations are passed to prevent Jews from associating with non-Jews and to punish those who do so. Based on these restrictions Otto and Gertrud could have been arrested.

1 This photo is exhibited in Berlin in 1935. The caption reads: "Two splendid Aryan children!" In fact these are Herbert Levy and his cousin Ellen-Eva, Jewish children....
2 Anne at a summer camp for city children in Laren, not far from Amsterdam, 1937.
3 The Nazis divide people according to "race." They believe that the "Aryan race" is superior. Here a child is being examined for "racial characteristics."

4 Anne, 1935, 1936, 1937.
5 Margot, 1935, 1936, 1937.
6 Grandma Frank (left) and Anne's Aunt Helene (center) at the Basel train station. By 1933, all of the immediate family of Anne's father have left Germany.

7

8

1935 – 1937

Hitler has two major goals: to create a "racially pure," superior German people and to form a Greater German Empire, which will require conquering vast new territories. The Nazis regard the Jews not only as an inferior people but also as dangerous. They labor under the illusion that "international Jewry" is a powerful force intent on destroying the so-called "Aryan race".

7 The Nazis' image of the "ideal" Aryan.

8 All of the media are called upon to promote anti-Semitic (anti-Jewish) propaganda. At this mass rally in Berlin on August 15, 1935, Julius Streicher, a prominent Nazi and publisher of the anti-Semitic newspaper "Der Stürmer" addresses the assembled 16,000 people on the "Jewish threat." The banners read "The Jews are our misfortune" and "Women and girls - the Jews are your ruination."

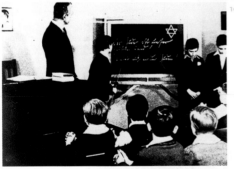

9 The public humiliation of Julius Wolff, a Jew, and his "Aryan" girlfriend Christine Reemann in the German town of Norden, July 22, 1935. The sign reads "I am a defiler of the race."

10 Jewish students standing in front of the class. The sign reads "The Jew is our greatest enemy! Watch out for the Jews!"

11 Racial examination of the gypsies. In addition to the Jews, other groups are also seen as a threat to the "pure Aryan race": gypsies, homosexuals and the handicapped.

"Our lives were not without anxiety"

"Our lives were not without anxiety, since our relatives in Germany were suffering under Hitler's anti-Jewish laws. After the pogroms in 1938 my two uncles (my mother's brothers) fled Germany, finding safe refuge in North America. My grandmother came to live with us. She was 73 years old at the time."

(ANNE FRANK)

1938 – 1939

Otto and Edith Frank become acquainted with other refugees from Germany. Among them are Hermann and Auguste van Pels, their son Peter, and Fritz Pfeffer, who will later join the Frank family in hiding. The Van Pels family fled Osnabrück in 1937. Hermann van Pels became Otto Frank's business partner. Like Anne's uncles, Fritz Pfeffer fled Germany after "Kristallnacht."

1. Anne celebrates her birthday with her friends on June 12, 1939.
2. Refugees on board the "St. Louis" in the Antwerp harbor, Belgium, June 17, 1939.
3. The synagogue in Frankfurt am Main in flames during "Kristall-nacht," Crystal Night or The Night of Broken Glass, November 9-10, 1938.
4. Grandma Holländer flees Germany in March 1939 and comes to Amsterdam to live with the Frank family. She dies in January 1942.

5. Peter van Pels (center) in 1936 with the Jewish Boy Scouts in Osnabrück, Germany.
6. Fritz Pfeffer with his non-Jewish fiancée, Charlotte Kaletta. Marriages between Jews and non-Jews have been forbidden by law in Germany since 1935. Couples who come to the Netherlands are still unable to marry because the Netherlands respects this aspect of German legislation.

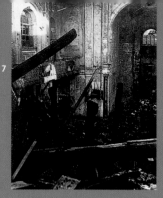

7

The list of restrictions imposed on the Jews of Germany keeps on growing, all to one purpose: to isolate the Jewish population from the non-Jewish population. The Nazis organize a pogrom against the Jews on the night of November 9-10, 1938. The immensity of the danger has become all too clear, and many Jews decide to flee Germany. But more and more countries are closing their borders to refugees.

7 The devastated interior
   of the Aachen synagogue.
   Anne's parents were
   married in this synagogue
   in 1925. The pogrom leaves
   177 synagogues destroyed,
   7,500 shops in ruins and
   236 Jews murdered. More
   than 30,000 Jews are
   arrested and taken to concentration camps.

8 Pedestrians on the
   Potsdamer Straße in Berlin
   looking at a shop in ruins
   on November 10th.

9 The arrest of Jews in
   Oldenburg, Germany, after
   "Kristallnacht."

10 Young Jewish refugees
   arriving in England,
   December 1938. In some
   cases children are granted
   asylum. Most of them will
   never see their parents
   again.

11 The arrival of Jewish children in Lisbon, Portugal,
   August 1941.

"You'll be next"
Hans Massaquoi

"I was six years old when I started school in 1932. The teachers who objected to the new regime were quickly replaced by younger pro-Nazi teachers. Some of them, including the principal, were plainly hostile to me and did their very best to insult me and to make contemptuous remarks about my race. One time - I must have been about ten - one of the teachers took me aside and said, 'When we've settled the score with the Jews, you'll be next.'"

"Cleansing" then

Because of the obsession to "purify" and "improve" the so-called Aryan race, many minority groups were no longer accepted in German society. Other groups that were targeted besides the Jews were the physically and mentally handicapped, homosexuals, gypsies and blacks. They were excluded from society, persecuted, and later often killed.

1   Hans Massaquoi,
     around 1930.
2   Hans Massaquoi

"Cleansing" now

The Nazis put their ideas about a "racially
pure" society into practice. Today in former
Yugoslavia, more than fifty years after World
War Two, people have translated words into
action with the same fervor. "Ethnic purity"
and "ethnic cleansing" have become
common expressions since the war in that
country began. This desire to "purify" society
of all those with a different culture, religion
or ethnic background is something that we
see in many parts of the world today.

"The trouble started for the Jews"

"After May 1940 the good times were few and far between: first there was the war, then the capitulation and then the arrival of the Germans, which is when the trouble started for the Jews."

(ANNE FRANK)

1939 – 1940

1 The Frank family on the Merwedeplein.
2 In September 1939 World War Two begins.
3 Warsaw, September 14, 1939. Polish children look on anxiously as German airplanes attack the city.

A few months after Anne's tenth birthday World War Two breaks out. Otto and Edith hope that the Netherlands will stay out of the war. But on May 10, 1940, the German army also invades the Netherlands.

4 June 1939. "Margot and I had just got out of the water and I still remember how terribly cold I was, that's why I put on my bathrobe, granny sitting there at the back so sweetly and peacefully." (Anne Frank)
5 Anne with Hannah Goslar, one of her best friends, May, 1940.
6 Anne, August 1940.

7

8

7 Heinrich Himmler, leader of the SS, in conversation with a Russian boy. "The fate of the Russians, Czechs and other Slavic peoples leaves me completely cold. Whether they live in prosperity or starve to death interests me only insofar as we can use them as slaves."

8 Behind the Polish front lines the terrorization of the Jews begins immediately. Jews are humiliated and beaten in the streets. The occupying forces organize pogroms in which thousands of Jews are killed.

1939·1940

On August 23, 1939, Germany signs a non-aggression pact with the Soviet Union. On September 1, 1939, Germany invades Poland. Large areas of the country are evacuated to make room for the German colonists who are to settle there. Many prominent Poles are murdered. In Western Europe little is known of the atrocities being committed in Poland. But in May, 1940, the war begins in the West as well: the Netherlands, Belgium and France are occupied by the German army. The Nazis regard Western Europeans as kindred peoples and spare them the kinds of atrocities that they perpetrated on the Poles. But the registration of the Jews in the Netherlands begins during the first year of the occupation.

9 The German army enters Amsterdam not far from Otto Frank's office building, May 16, 1940.

10 After a speedy victory in the Netherlands, Belgium and France, the German troops are enthusiastically welcomed back to Berlin, July 18, 1940.

11 Initially the Nazis try to win over the Dutch population to their ideology. Only a small portion actively collaborate with the occupiers during the war. Most people try to adjust to the new situation. But as the war years pass, aversion to the occupying power and resistance against it increase.

"A series of anti-Jewish decrees"

"Our freedom was severely restricted by a series of anti-Jewish decrees: Jews were required to wear a yellow star; Jews were required to turn in their bicycles; Jews were forbidden to use streetcars; Jews were forbidden to ride in cars, even their own; Jews were required to do their shopping between 3 and 5 p.m.; Jews were required to frequent only Jewish-owned barbershops and beauty parlors; Jews were forbidden to be out on the streets between 8 p.m. and 6 a.m. (...)"

(ANNE FRANK)

1941 – 1942

1

2

3

4

1 Anne at the Montessori
  School, 1941.
2 In Germany and in most
  of the occupied territories,
  the Jews have to wear a
  yellow Star of David.
3 All children over six are
  forced to wear a yellow
  Star of David.
4 From now on, Jews have
  to go to special "Jewish"
  schools. "I'd been accepted
  at the Jewish Lyceum,
  where Margot also went
  to school." (Anne Frank)
5 On July 16, 1941, Miep,
  Otto Frank's secretary,
  marries Jan Gies. Otto and
  Anne walking with the
  other wedding guests.
6 Johannes Kleiman and
  Victor Kugler, employees
  of Otto Frank, in front
  of the office on the
  Prinsengracht.

Jewish children have to go to separate
schools. Anne and Margot begin attending
the Jewish Lyceum. Everywhere you turn
there are signs that say "No Jews allowed."
Jews are also no longer permitted to own
their own businesses, so Otto Frank names
Johannes Kleiman as director of his
company while continuing to be active
behind the scenes. The business is given a
different name as well, Gies & Co., after Jan
Gies, Miep's husband.

5

6

1941 – 1942

7 The first open confrontation between the occupying forces and the Dutch population occurs in February 1941. A razzia is held in Amsterdam where 421 Jewish men are rounded up and transported to the Mauthausen concentration camp. In protest the population of Amsterdam goes on strike, but after two days the strike is crushed by the occupiers.

8

8 Protesting against Nazi policy is just as dangerous in Germany. Only a few can summon up the courage. A group of German students known as "Die Weisse Rose" begin distributing pamphlets. They are betrayed and some members are sentenced to death in 1943. A quote from one of their pamphlets reads, "We will not keep silent. We are your bad conscience: The White Rose will not let you rest!"

In all the occupied countries, one of the first regulations imposed by the German occupying force is the registration of the Jews. The next step is isolation. With increasing speed, more and more new regulations are enacted against the Jews aimed at separating them from the non-Jewish population. The strategy is effective: many non-Jews no longer dare associate with Jews and vice-versa. In June 1941, Germany invades the Soviet Union. The United States and Japan also become involved in the war.

9 German soldiers look on at the hanging of Russian partisans. Schlobin, January 1942.

10 In Eastern Europe the German army quickly moves forward after the invasion of the Soviet Union in 1941. The advancing army is reinforced by special commando units (Einsatsgruppen) who are instructed to kill as many Jews, gypsies and partisans as possible. It is estimated that within one year, one and a half million men, women and children are executed.

11 Vinnitsa, Ukraine, 1942. A Jewish man is executed with a shot in the back of the neck on the edge of a mass grave. Top Nazi officials are now seeking faster and more efficient methods of extermination.

"Margot has to report"

"On Sunday morning Hello and I lay on our balcony in the sun, on Sunday afternoon he was going to come back, but at about 3 o'clock a policeman arrived and called from the door downstairs, Miss Margot Frank. Mummy went down and the policeman gave her a card which said that Margot Frank has to report to the S.S."

(ANNE FRANK)

1942

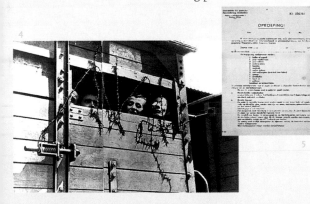

On June 12, 1942, Anne is given a diary for her birthday. A few weeks later, on July 5, 1942, Margot receives a call-up notice. The call-up does not come as a total surprise to Anne's parents. Since the spring of 1941, Otto Frank has been making preparations to go into hiding with his family in the "Secret Annex," an empty storage area at the back of his office building on the Prinsengracht. Only his closest office staff know of this plan. After the call-up arrives, the decision is made to go into hiding immediately. Miep Gies comes that evening to help bring clothes and other items to the hiding place.

1 This is the last known photo taken of Anne and Margot.

2 Deportation from the Muiderpoort train station, Amsterdam, May 25, 1943.

3 "I hope I will be able to confide everything to you, as I have never been able to confide in anyone, and I hope you will be a great source of comfort and support." (Anne Frank)

4 People are packed together in cattle cars and carried off to unknown destinations, traveling for days without food or water.

5 The call-up notice. "I was stunned. A call-up: everyone knows what that means. Visions of concentration camps and lonely cells raced through my head (...)." (Anne Frank)

By the end of 1941, the isolation and registration of the Jews in Germany and in most of the occupied territories is complete. During the "Wannsee Conference" in Berlin on January 20, 1942, top Nazi officials put the finishing touches on the "Final Solution to the Jewish question" (Endlösung der udenfrage). They are intent on murdering all eleven million European Jews. Plans for deportation and annihilation will now be carried out. As 1942 continues, deportations to concentration and extermination camps get underway. Most of these camps are in Poland.

6
7

1942

6   Adolf Eichmann, one of the participants at the "Wannsee Conference," is responsible for organizing the deportation of all the Jews of Europe to concentration and extermination camps.

7   The deportation of the Jewish inhabitants of Hanau, Germany, May 30, 1941.

8   The deportation of Dutch Jews, 1942.

9   In the summer of 1942, the Nazis begin the evacuation of the Warsaw ghetto. The ghetto inhabitants are transported directly to the extermination camps. In April 1943, the remaining inhabitants of the ghetto rise up in revolt. Under abominable conditions, they hold out against the superior force of the Germans for twenty-eight days.

10 In September 1940, a separate sealed district is created in Warsaw in which 500,000 Jews are forced to live: the ghetto. The living conditions are horrendous. Cold, hunger and infectious diseases run rampant. By the summer of 1942 more than 100,000 people have died there.

"I am not a hero"
Miep Gies

"Otto Frank took a breath and asked, 'Miep are you willing to take on the responsibility of taking care of us while we are in hiding?'
'Of course,' I answered. "There is a look between two people once or twice in a lifetime that cannot be described by words. That look passed between us.
"I am not a hero. There is nothing special about me. I was only willing to do what was asked of me and what seemed necessary at the time."

Helping then

During the war, Jews were often dependent on non-Jews for help, but only a small portion of the non-Jewish population actively offered their assistance. Most people remained passive. That small active group consisted of very ordinary people whose decision to help, under extremely difficult circumstances, made them extraordinary.

Helping now

Today many people live in peace. The choice to stand up for someone is rarely a matter of life or death. Nevertheless, at one time or another we all find ourselves in situations in which people are threatened because of the color of their skin, their convictions or their beliefs. To speak up or take action at such a time, when others remain silent and do nothing, is a real sign of courage and humanity. This kind of support is still vitally important.

1 Miep Gies.
2 Miep Gies, around 1940.

July 6, 1942 – 1944 August 4,

1 The office building on the Prinsengracht. At the back is the "Secret Annex," the hiding place.

2 The front of the office building located at 263 Prinsengracht (center), shortly after the war.

3 The Secret Annex, the hiding place, photographed from the back yard.
1. Anne's and Fritz Pfeffer's room
2. Otto, Edith and Margot Frank's room
3. Hermann and Auguste van Pels's room
4. the attic

4 A revolving bookcase conceals the entrance to the Secret Annex.

"An ideal place to hide in"

"The Annex is an ideal place to hide in. It may be damp and lopsided, but there's probably not a more comfortable hiding place in all of Amsterdam. No, in all of Holland."

(ANNE FRANK)

On July 6, 1942, the Frank family go into hiding. Later they will be joined by the Van Pels family and Fritz Pfeffer. For more than two years, these eight people live in the Annex shut off from the outside world. It is a time full of anxiety and tension as well as boredom. Otto Frank's closest office staff supply them with food, clothing and books.

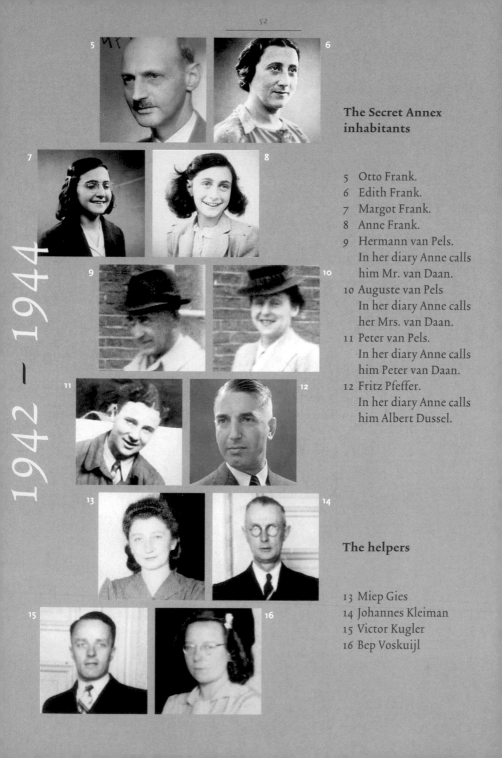

1942 ~ 1944

The Secret Annex inhabitants

5 Otto Frank.
6 Edith Frank.
7 Margot Frank.
8 Anne Frank.
9 Hermann van Pels.
   In her diary Anne calls
   him Mr. van Daan.
10 Auguste van Pels
   In her diary Anne calls
   her Mrs. van Daan.
11 Peter van Pels.
   In her diary Anne calls
   him Peter van Daan.
12 Fritz Pfeffer.
   In her diary Anne calls
   him Albert Dussel.

The helpers

13 Miep Gies
14 Johannes Kleiman
15 Victor Kugler
16 Bep Voskuijl

"Up to now our bedroom, with its blank walls, was very bare. Thanks to Father - who brought my entire postcard and movie-star collection here beforehand - and to a brush and a pot of glue, I was able to plaster the walls with pictures." (Anne Frank)

17 After the arrest, the whole Secret Annex is stripped by order of the Nazi occupiers. Only a few things are left behind, among them the pictures that Anne pasted

on her wall. This is the room that was shared by Anne Frank and Fritz Pfeffer. It is shown here after being temporarily refurnished based on information provided by Miep Gies and others.

"Not being able to go outside upsets me more than I can say, and I'm terrified our hiding place will be discovered and that we'll be shot. That, of course, is a fairly dismal prospect." (Anne Frank)

1942 – 1944

"I feel wicked sleeping in a warm bed, while somewhere out there my dearest friends are dropping from exhaustion or being knocked to the ground. I get frightened myself when I think of close friends who are now at the mercy of the cruelest monsters ever to stalk the earth. And all because they're Jews." (Anne Frank)

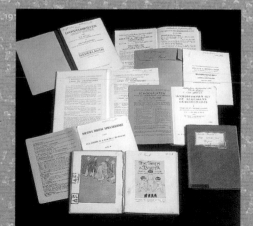

18 The storage attic
19 Text books that were used
   in the Secret Annex.
20 The stairway in Peter's
   room leading up to the
   attic.

"Miep has so much to carry she looks like a pack mule. She goes forth nearly every day to scrounge up vegetables, and then bicycles back with her purchases in large shopping bags. She's also the one who brings five library books with her every Saturday. We long for Saturday because that means books. We're like a bunch of little kids with a present. Ordinary people don't know how much books can mean to someone who's cooped up. Our only diversions are reading, studying and listening to the radio." (Anne Frank)

Every day, Margot, Peter and Anne spend several hours on their schoolwork. They hope the war will be over quickly and that they'll be able to return to school. Otto Frank helps them with their lessons.

"I loathe algebra, geometry and arithmetic. I enjoy all my other school subjects, but history's my favorite!" (Anne Frank)

21

1942 1944

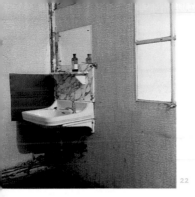

"Father, Mother and Margot still can't get used to the chiming of the Westertoren clock, which tells us the time every quarter of an hour. Not me, I liked it from the start; it sounds so reassuring, especially at night." (Anne Frank)

"If it's that bad in Holland, what must it be like in those faraway and uncivilized places where the Germans are sending them? We assume that most of them are being murdered. The English radio says they're being gassed. Perhaps that's the quickest way to die. I feel terrible." (Anne Frank)

"It's twice as hard for us young people to hold on to our opinions at a time when ideals are being shattered and destroyed, when the worst side of human nature predominates, when everyone has come to doubt truth, justice and God." (Anne Frank)

Before long Anne fills up the diary that she was given for her thirteenth birthday, so she begins using notebooks, old ledgers and loose sheets of paper for recording her thoughts. On March 29, 1944, she hears an announcement on the English radio that after the war there will be a collection of diaries. She decides to edit all her diary entries.

"The nice part is being able to write down all my thoughts and feelings; otherwise, I'd absolutely suffocate." (Anne Frank)

21 The Westertoren as seen from the attic window.
22 The washroom.
23 Anne Frank's writings.

"Why are millions spent on the war each day, while not a penny is available for medical science, artists or the poor? Why do people have to starve when mountains of food are rotting away in other parts of the world? Oh, why are people so crazy?" (Anne Frank)

"Will this year, 1944, bring us victory? We don't know yet. But where there's hope, there's life. It fills us with fresh courage and makes us strong again. (...) Oh, Kitty, the best part about the invasion is that I have the feeling that friends are on the way. (...) Maybe, Margot says, I can even go back to school in October or September." (Anne Frank)

24 Hermann and Auguste van Pels's room.
25 List of deportees on the last transport from Westerbork to Auschwitz, September 3, 1944.

Anne writes in her diary for the last time on August 1, 1944. On August 4th, a beautiful summer day, the inhabitants are arrested. They've been betrayed. Until this very day no one knows who betrayed them. Four Dutch Nazis under the leadership of Karl Silberbauer, an Austrian Nazi, burst into the office building. Silberbauer grabs a briefcase and shakes out its contents to make room for the family's cash and valuables. Anne's diary entries fall to the ground. A few hours later they are found there by Miep and Bep.

Four days later, the prisoners arrive at Westerbork transit camp. On September 3, 1944, the last transport train leaves the Netherlands bound for Auschwitz. Among the more than one thousand people on board are the eight inhabitants of the Secret Annex.

Häftlinge

551. Oppenheimer-Levy	Juliane	22.2.69	ohne
552. Orlem-Polak	Elias	8.4.13	Stenotypistin
553. Rijssman	Philip	15.4.01	Kaufmann
554. v.Fels	Clara	27.5.20	Kinderpflegerin
555. van Fels	Herman	21.3.90	Besch.Kaufmann
556. van Fels-Boettgen	Auguste	20.2.90	ohne
557. v.. .le	Peter	4.11.26	Metallarb.
558. Peffer Dr.	Fritz	8.4.89	...arzt
559. Pino	Pietje	17.10.01	...
560. Polak	Hans	2.4.1.	
561. Polak			
562. Polak-Wessel			

Häftlinge

301. Engers	Isidor	30.4.93	Kaufmann
302. Engers	Leonard	13.6.20	Landarbeiter
303. Engers	Manfred	1.5.05	Verleger
304. Franco	Arthur	27.8.81	Kaufmann
305. Frank	Isaac	29.11.87	Installateur
306. Frank	Margot	16.2.26	ohne
307. Frank	Otto	12.5.89	Kaufmann
308. Frank-Hollender	Edith	16.1.00	ohne
309. Frank	Anneliese	12.6.29	ohne
310. v.Franck	Sara	27.4.02	Typistin
311. Franken	Abraham	16.5.96	Landarbeiter
312. Franken-Beyand	Johanna	24.12.96	Landbauer
313. Franken	Herman	12.5.34	ohne
314. Franken	Louis	10.8.17	Gärtner
315. Franken	Rosalina	29.3.27	Landbau
316. Frankfort	Alex	14.11.19	Dr.i.d.Oekonomie
317. Frankfort-Elsas	Regina	11.12.19	Apoth.-Ass.
318. Frankfoort	Elias	22.10.98	Schneider
319. Frankfort	Max	20.8.21	Schneider
320. Frankfort-Weyl	Betty	25.3.24	Näherin
321. Frankfort-Werkendam	Roxette	24.6.98	Schriftstellerin
	Herman	22.6.87	Hochschullehrer
322. Frijda	Henriette	28.4.21	Typistin
323. Frenk	Rosa	15.3.24	Haushalthilfe
324. Frenk	Isaac	10.3.20	Korrespondent
325. Friezer			
326. Fruitman-Vleeschdrager	Fanny	24.1.03	ohne
	Elie	24.10.03	Betriebleiter
327. Gans	Gesina	20.12.05	Maschinenstrickerin
328. Gans-Koopman	Kalman	6.3.79	Diamentbearb.
329. Gans	Klara	12.5.13	Näherin
330. Gans-Nord	Paul	27.9.08	Landbauer
331. Gans	Abraham	9.11.78	Metzger
332. v.Gelder	Reintje	22.10.81	ohne
333. v.Gelder-de Jong	Alexander	27.8.03	Kaufmann
334. v.Gelder			
335. v.Gelder-Vischscharper	Clara	12.4.12	ohne
	Hendrika	17.3.77	ohne
336. v.Gelder-Raphael	Henny	19.5.18	Näherin
337. v.Gelder	Sion	19.5.19	Landarbeiter
338. v.Gelder	Johanna	22.5.10	Verkäuferin
339. v.Gelderen	Karel	25.8.99	Kapellmeister
340. v.Gelderen	Alexander	1.5.69	ohne
341. Gerson	Kaatje	9.9.94	ohne
342. Gerson-Hertog	Arthur	24.3.27	Bäcker
343. Ginsberg	Benjamin	7.9.93	Kaufmann
344. Ginsberg	Rosa	10.6.97	ohne
345. Ginsberg-Rosen	Israel	3.5.94	Stepper
346. Glowinski	Sara	31.12.91	Näherin
347. Glowinski-Streep	Zadok	6.3.79	Diamantarb.
348. Gobets	Berner	26.9.15	Kaufmann
349. Godschalk	Hans	6.6.10	Pelzsortierer
350. Goldberg			

A few of the major concentration and extermination
camps.

▲ Concentration camp

ⓘ Extermination camp

▴ Camps where the people from
the Secret Annex were imprisoned

26 In March 1945, 28,000
people die in Bergen-
Belsen of hunger, cold
and disease.

27 During the last six months
before its liberation the
Bergen-Belsen camp is
badly overcrowded. Most of
the prisoners are women.

26

1944 – 1945

The inhabitants of the Secret Annex

When Auschwitz is evacuated, **Peter van Pels** is forced to join in the long and brutal march to the Mauthausen concentration camp. He dies there on May 5, 1945, three days before the camp is liberated.

In October 1944, **Auguste van Pels** is taken from Auschwitz to Bergen-Belsen along with Anne and Margot. She remains in that camp for only a brief period. In the spring of 1945 she is taken via Buchenwald to Theresienstadt, where she dies.

Hermann van Pels is gassed at Auschwitz.

Fritz Pfeffer is transported from Auschwitz to Neuengamme. He dies there on December 20, 1944.

In early October 1944, **Edith Frank** is separated from her daughters. She stays behind in Auschwitz and dies there on January 6, 1945.

Margot Frank, together with Anne and Auguste van Pels, is taken from Auschwitz to Bergen-Belsen in October 1944. At the end of March she dies of typhus.

Anne Frank is transported from Auschwitz to Bergen-Belsen with Margot and Auguste van Pels in October 1944. Like her sister Margot, Anne Frank dies there of typhus. Her death occurs a few days after Margot's.

Otto Frank survives the Auschwitz concentration camp. At the end of January 1945 he is freed by the Russians. After a long, roundabout journey of more than four months he returns to Amsterdam.

Helpers

Bep Voskuijl and **Miep Gies** are not arrested after the raid, but the two men, **Johannes Kleiman** and **Victor Kugler**, are both taken prisoner. They are brought to a camp in the Netherlands. All the helpers survive the war.

"It wasn't the same Anne"

Hannah Goslar

"We saw each other once again in Bergen-Belsen... It wasn't the same Anne. She was a broken girl... it was so terrible. She immediately began to cry, and she told me: 'I don't have any parents any more...' I always think, if Anne had known that her father was still alive, she might have had more strength to survive."

Anne's school friend Hannah is in another part of Bergen-Belsen when Anne and Margot arrive there. She speaks with Anne through the barbed-wire fence separating them.

"She thought that her father had been gassed because he was no longer a young man. She told me about the gas chamber. I didn't know anything about it. There were rumors, but how can you believe such things?"

"'I don't have anyone any more,' she said. Her sister was dying - Anne knew that, because everyone who had typhus died."

Hannah Goslar and her sister Rachel both survived Bergen-Belsen. It wasn't until after the liberation, when Hannah lay in a hospital recovering from typhus, that she learned of Anne's death.

"Six million people were killed. What is six million? It's impossible to comprehend a number like that. But if you read the part of Anne's diary in which she writes about me, and then you see me here, her friend, only six months older than she was, that might make it easier to imagine."

Hannah Pick-Goslar now lives in Israel.

1 Hannah Goslar (right) and
  Anne Frank, May 1940.
2 Hannah Pick-Goslar

"I was just lucky"
Janina Bauman

"If I had known Anne during the war I would have envied her. She didn't have to wander the streets in search of food or a place to hide. Her refuge was a relatively safety one. Her father was with her, I'm certainly jealous of that. The fact that I survived and she didn't is a cruel accident - I was just lucky."

Janina Bauman is a Jewish girl from Poland. She is thirteen years old when World War Two breaks out, one year older than Anne Frank. Janina, her mother and her little sister Sophie are confined to the Warsaw ghetto. In July 1942 the Nazis' evacuation of the ghetto begins. The Jews living there are transported to Treblinka and murdered.

"We went into hiding. For six months we hid in dark, wet cellars, in dusty attics, in the spaces behind heavy furniture, in ruins and under piles of rubble. The ghetto grew smaller and smaller, our situation more and more dangerous.
"We escaped from the trap. It was terribly dangerous. Jews who were found outside the ghetto were killed, as were Poles who helped or hid Jews. People who betrayed a Jew in hiding were given a handsome reward.

"We were on the run for two years. All sorts of people risked their lives and the lives of their families to save us, including a drug addict, a prostitute, an occultist and a priest. And every time we would have to leave because someone threatened to betray us. So we encountered cruel and corrupt people as well as very brave and honest people. My life was saved by Poles, not once but over and over again.

"I lived in Poland until 1968. Because of the anti-Semitism there, I emigrated to England. I've written a book about my life, 'Winter in the Morning.' It's extremely important to me that the world know that history is not just a matter of black and white."

1   Janina Bauman
2   Janina Bauman, 1943.

Most of the Jews of Western Europe, including those in the Netherlands, have no idea what is in store for them. They're summoned to report for so-called "work camps" in Eastern Europe. Some news does leak out about what is happening in the camps, but most of the Jews find these stories so incredible that they report anyway. One of the few ways to escape deportation is to go into hiding, but those who do so, and those who help them, risk harsh punishment at the hands of the Nazis. In addition, you have to have both money and non-Jewish contacts to find a place to hide. Few Jews succeed in finding a safe haven. Few non-Jews offer their help.

3

3 The circumstances under which people go into hiding are different for everyone. Most families are split up, and count-less individuals wander from place to place, completely dependent on the help of others.

4 It's a bit easier to find a hiding place for children than for adults. Many children never see their parents again.

4

5

5 Their hiding place discovered, a group of people are arrested.

6 Dutch people are also active in the resistance. Some of them forge identification papers.

7 A "receipt" issued for turning in five Jews. The person who betrayed them is given 37.50 in guilders, about one week's salary. In the Netherlands, one-third of those who go into hiding are discovered and deported. Betrayal is often involved, as in the case of the eight who hid in the Secret Annex. People betrayed Jews for many different reasons: anti-Semitism, a sense of duty or financial gain.

"We were just like nocturnal animals"

Hannes Weiss

"There was a big razzia, and many of our family members were picked up and taken to Auschwitz. We escaped and went into hiding. Then there was another razzia. We hid under the floorboards, and they shot right through the floor. "Then we took to the road. We were just like nocturnal animals: walking all night and hiding during the daytime."

Hannes Weiss is fourteen years old in 1944, one year younger than Anne Frank.
"It was different back then. People would yell, 'Black gypsy, dirty gypsy.' Terrible! Then the doctors came. I was just a kid. They examined us: studied how you walked, measured everything, just so they could determine what a gypsy was. We didn't know what it was all about. Later on we did: all the gypsies had to be killed. Mother and father were terrified. That's when they left Germany.

"We went into hiding, but we were betrayed. People would do anything for money. We were taken by train to camp Westerbork. While we were standing on the train platform the policeman who was guarding us said, 'When I take my hat off, run!' I guess you realize that we didn't wait for the hat. We were off in a flash!

"It's been more than fifty years since the war, but there's still discrimination. The Nazis tried to annihilate our people. I want to do everything I can to keep us alive."

1   Hannes Weiss.

Hannes Weiss survived the war. Many
members of his family did not. He now lives
in the Netherlands and has set up an associ-
ation for gypsies.

2

2 By 1936 the "Rassenhygi-
enische Forschungsstelle"
has already been set up.
Its job: to track down and
register all gypsies on the
basis of "racial characteristics."

3 The deportation of gypsies
from Hohenasperg, a
transit camp near
Stuttgart, May 18, 1940.

3

The Nazis regarded the gypsies, like the Jews, as a threat to the so-called "pure Aryan blood." Gypsies are examined for "racial characteristics," registered and deported to concentration camps. Between 200,000 and 500,000 gypsies from all over Europe are murdered by the Nazis.

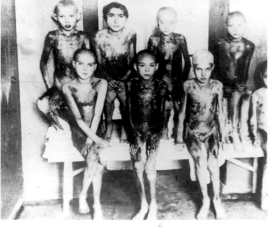

4 About forty gypsy children are brought to the "St. Josefspflege" in Mulfingen, Germany, for so-called "racial studies." Their parents are deported and gassed. In 1944 the Nazis move the children from the "St. Josefspflege" to Auschwitz. Most of them are gassed there. Others are forced to undergo medical experiments.

5 Settela Steinbach, a gypsy girl, being deported from the Netherlands to Auschwitz, May 15, 1944.

6 Only a few survive the medical experiments carried out by Dr. Joseph Mengele and other Nazi doctors in the camps.

"Today I can say it: 'Gassed'"

Ruth Wallage-Binheim

"After arriving in Auschwitz, my sister Hanna and I survived the selection. Our heads were shaved and numbers were tattooed on our arms. Then we asked the other prisoners about our mother, Frieda Binheim, who we knew had been taken to Auschwitz. They looked at us: didn't we understand? Then they looked up, at the sky.

"Later we did the same thing. When newcomers asked us about their family members we just looked up. It's a word that you couldn't utter. It's still hard, even now. Today I can say it: 'Gassed.' Because that's what happened!"

In 1939 Ruth Binheim is thirteen years old, the same age as Margot Frank. She flees from Germany to the Netherlands with her brother and sister. Her parents are not given a visa. In 1942 the deportations in the Netherlands begin and Ruth and her sister are deported to Auschwitz.

"I got very sick one time. I had jaundice and I couldn't stand up. Thanks to Hanna, who supported me, I was able to stand during the roll call. If you were sick you were not included in the count. You were sent to the infirmary. That was the end of you - we knew that.

"At one point a small group of us women were brought to another camp. The stench there was awful, terrible! The next morning I said, 'I had such a dreadful dream! I heard people screaming, so penetrating, so frightening, a whole bunch of people at the same time. The screams became fewer and fewer until I could only hear one or two ...' But it had really happened: Right near us, in the woods, people had been burned alive in a big pit... Then we immediately knew where the stench had come from.

"We had to open the backpacks belonging to the people who had been gassed and sort out their belongings - the dresses, the jackets and so forth. These things were sent to the German population as 'Liebesgaben' (gifts).

"If Hanna and I got a chunk of bread we always shared it. If I divided it I gave her the bigger piece, and vice versa. I think that had to do with our will to survive. If Hanna and I had not had each other, we would have not survived."

1 Ruth Wallage-Binheim
2 Ruth (left) and her sister, Hanna, 1946.

Ruth and Hanna survived the death march from Auschwitz to Ravensbrück and were liberated at Camp Retzov by the Russians. Their parents and their brother did not survive the camps.

3 As soon as they arrive in
   the extermination camps
   people are divided up.
   Pregnant women, children
   under fifteen, old people
   and the sick are usually
   gassed on the same day
   and cremated. The others
   are forced into exhausting
   hard labor.
4 Hungarian Jews on the
   platform at Auschwitz,
   selected for the gas
   chamber.

The Nazis build extermination camps: camps that are especially equipped to kill large numbers of people as quickly as possible. Even when the fortunes of war turn, the extermination continues at a rapid rate. The goal is to kill all eleven million Jews in Europe.

5 The registration of a young woman after her arrival at Auschwitz. Most prisoners have a number tattooed on their arms.

6 May 1944. Recently arrived female prisoners are taken away to have their heads shaved.

7 Poison gas cylinders (Zyklon-B) that are used in the gas chambers.

"I've lost everything, except my life"
Otto Frank

"And I'll never forget the time in Auschwitz when seventeen-year-old Peter van Pels and I saw a group of selected men. Among those men was Peter's father. The men marched away. Two hours later a truck came by loaded with their clothing."

With the approach of the Red Army the Nazis hastily abandon Auschwitz. Otto is left behind in the infirmary.

On March 18, 1945, Otto writes a letter from Poland to his cousin Milly in Great Britain: "We were freed by the Russians on January 27. I had the good fortune to be staying in the camp infirmary then, which was not destroyed by the Germans. They tried to take me along when they fled the camp, but I managed to escape and stayed behind. I thought that this was my only chance. I don't know how many of my comrades who were forced to go with them are still alive. It can't be many."

"We're waiting here for repatriation, but the war is still on and we're far from home. Holland is still partially occupied."

Katiovice, 18.14.1945

Dear Milly,

I hope, that this letter will reach you, giving you the news, that I am living. It really is a wonder. I wrote to Robert and Paul, but it is not certain, that my letters will arrive, so I ask

"I know nothing about Edith and the children. When we arrived in Birkenau-Auschwitz on September 5th we were separated.
"I've lost everything, except my life. There's nothing left of my family, no photo, no letter from my children, nothing - nothing."

On June 3, 1945, Otto Frank returns to Amsterdam. It later turns out that the family photo albums and his daughter Anne's diary have been saved after all.

1 The letter to Milly Stanfield, March 18, 1945.
2 Otto Frank
3 Otto Frank, shortly after the war.

As the Allied troops grow closer the Nazis
try to eradicate all traces of their crimes. On
January 17, 1945, the SS evacuate Auschwitz
after having blown up the gas chambers and
the crematoria. The guards force the 50,000
surviving prisoners, among which Peter van
Pels, to march to camps that lie further
from the front. Only a few survive these
"death marches."

4 The survivors of the
   Auschwitz infirmary
   with their Russian
   liberators.
5 Prisoners of the
   Buchenwald concentra-
   tion camp. In the second
   row from the bottom,
   seventh from the left, is
   Elie Wiesel, who will
   later become a famous
   writer and winner of the
   Nobel Prize. "In those
   times, one climbed to the
   summit of humanity by
   simply remaining
   human." (Elie Wiesel)
6 Auschwitz-Birkenau

"It is not true that six million Jews were murdered; one Jew was murdered, six million times over."
(Abel Herzberg)

"After the war..."

"In any case, after the war I'd like to publish a book called The Secret Annex. It remains to be seen whether I'll succeed, but my diary can serve as the basis."

(ANNE FRANK)

1945

Otto Frank fulfills his daughter's wish. On June 3, 1945, after a roundabout journey, he arrives in Amsterdam and goes directly to the home of Miep and Jan Gies. Otto knows his wife has died, but he still has hope for Anne and Margot. Two months later Otto learns that both his daughters are dead. It is then that Miep hands the diary entries over to him. Otto reads them and is both moved and surprised. This was a side of his daughter that he had not known.

Friends urge him to have the diary published. It is difficult for Otto Frank to find a publisher, but finally, in June 1947, "Het Achterhuis" ("The Secret Annex") appears in an edition of 1,500 copies.

1 Frankfurt am Main, 1946.
2 Otto Frank (left) goes to live with Miep and Jan Gies and their son. In 1952 Otto remarries and moves to Basel, Switzerland.3 Anne Frank's writings.
4 Otto Frank hopes to obtain information about the fate of his daughters by placing an advertisement in the newspaper (August 1, 1945).
5 A letter testifying to the deaths of Margot and Anne Frank, written by Janny Brandes-Brilleslijper and delivered to Otto Frank in 1946.
6 The first edition of the diary, 1947.

After 1945

7   The liberation celebra-
tions in Eindhoven, the
Netherlands, 1944.
8   Life resumes its normal
course. Berlin, 1945.

The war is over. The few Jews who return from the camps or come out of hiding discover that almost all their family and friends are dead. The incomprehension and persistent anti-Semitism that they often encounter make their return bitterly disappointing.

War crimes tribunals are held in Nuremberg, Tokyo and other cities.

9 War crimes tribunal, November 1945. Reba Levy of Lithuania identifies her guard from the concentration camp at Dachau.

10 Summer 1945. A Jewish woman returning from a concentration camp is reunited with her child. In the ravages of Berlin she searches for the home that has been assigned to her.

11 A returning ex-prisoner at the Amsterdam train station.

"Therefore it is impossible for me to see it"

"For me this play is a part of my life, and the idea that my wife and children as well as I will be presented on the stage is a painful one to me. Therefore it is impossible for me to come and see it."

(OTTO FRANK)

After 1945

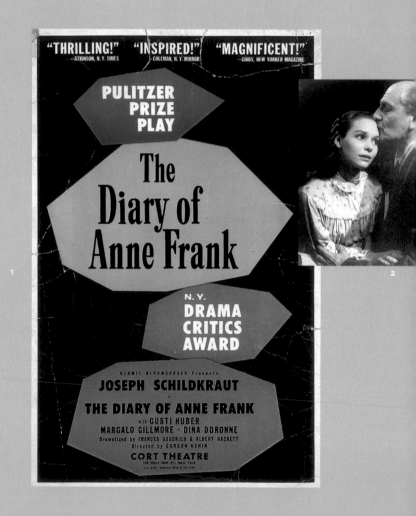

In 1955 in the United States the diary is adapted for the stage. The production is a huge success. It is followed by a feature-length film that is shown in packed theaters all over the world. Both the play and the film emphasize Anne Frank's hope and vitality. Millions of people read her diary, and many want to see for themselves the place where the diary of Anne Frank was written. In 1957 the former hiding place is saved from demolition, and in 1960 the house is first opened to the public.

1 Announcement of the play.
2 A scene from the premiere of the play.
3 The diary is translated into 55 languages; around 20 million copies of the book are sold; streets and schools are named after Anne Frank.
4 Otto Frank with the authors and the director of the play, in Anne's room.
5 Otto and his second wife, Fritzi, with Millie Perkins, who plays Anne in the film.
6 The house that had been a hiding place for Anne, her family and a few friends is opened as a small museum in 1960.

After 1945

7

8

7   In 1948 the Universal
    Declaration of Human
    Rights is enacted. Almost
    all the countries of the
    world commit themselves
    to respecting human
    rights. But the reality is
    often quite a different
    story.
8   In Germany, Paul Hahn
    (right) was persecuted
    during the Nazi period
    because of his homosexu-
    ality. On the basis of the
    same legislation, he is once
    again imprisoned after
    the war. In many other
    countries the views and
    legislation regarding
    homosexuality long
    remain unchanged.

The years after the war are devoted to reconstruction and plans for the future. There is little interest in looking back. The survivors suppress the memories of their traumatic experiences. Many Jews no longer want to live in Europe and decide to emigrate, with Israel and the United States as their primary destinations. Sometimes anti-Semitism plays a role in their decision. Prejudice and discrimination against other minority groups do not seem to have disappeared either.

9 A policeman removes a swastika from a New York synagogue, 1960.
10 Countless survivors, such as this gypsy woman, must learn to live with their terrible memories.
11 Holocaust survivors arriving in Haifa, 1947. Between 1944 and 1948, more than 200,000 Jewish Holocaust survivors from eastern and central Europe emigrate to Palestine. In 1948 the state of Israel is proclaimed.

"I answer them as well as I can"

"I have received many thousands of letters. Young people especially always want to know how these terrible things could ever have happened. I answer them as well as I can, and I often finish by saying: 'I hope that Anne's book will have an effect on the rest of your life so that insofar as it is possible in your circumstances, you will work for unity and peace.'"

(OTTO FRANK)

After 1945

1

1 Otto Frank, 1967.
2 Statue of Anne Frank in Utrecht, the Netherlands, 1983.
3 Publications denying the authenticity of Anne Frank's diary and the historicity of the Holocaust continue to appear.
4 President Nelson Mandela at the opening of the exhibition "Anne Frank in the World" in South Africa: "Some of us read Anne Frank's diary on Robben Island and derived much encouragement of it."

Otto Frank dedicates his life to carrying out his daughter Anne's ideals. He emphasizes the importance of mutual respect between people with different backgrounds. The international success of the diary provokes neo-Nazis to claim that it is a forgery, and out of sheer necessity Otto Frank is forced to take the matter to court.
A scientific examination carried out in 1986 provides conclusive proof of the diary's authenticity. Otto Frank dies in 1980 at the age of ninety. His daughter's diary is still being read by vast numbers of people.

After 1945

5

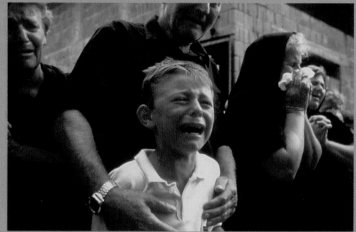

6

5 The "Russian National Unity Party" is one of the dozens of small extreme nationalist parties in Russia. Their supporters advocate the "genetic cleansing" of the Russian people.

6 A Croatian boy at the funeral of his father. Ethnic violence in former Yugoslavia; this is not the only country where such incidents have occurred during the 1990s.

In many countries there has been a sharp increase in extreme nationalism in the last ten years, often accompanied by discrimination and violence against minorities.

All countries have their minorities. Nearly every country has complied with international agreements providing equal treatment to all its citizens and protecting them against discrimination and racism. Whether these laws are actually enforced depends not only on the particular government but also on the effort of each individual citizen.

7 Roman Herzog, President of Germany: "On April 11 she wrote in her diary: 'One day this terrible war will be over. The time will come when we'll be people again and not just Jews!' In place of 'not just Jews,' Anne Frank could also have written: not just gypsies, not just Christians, not just trade union members, not just Socialists, not just the handicapped, not just this or that minority. It is our responsibility to see that people are never again divided up and selected in this way."

8 A demonstration of Swedish neo-Nazis. An angry woman lights into them with her purse.

Sources of photographs

Cover:
AFF/AFS
p. 6:
1: AFF/AFS
2: AFS
pp. 8-9:
1: AFF/AFS
2: AFF/AFS
3: IS
4: PC
5: PC
6: PC
pp. 10-11:
7: LBB
8: RIOD
9: AKG
10: RIOD
11: IS
pp. 12-13:
1: AFF/AFS
2: BPK
3: AKG
4: AFF/AFS
5: AFF/AFS
6: AFF/AFS
pp. 14-15:
7: AKG
8: LBB
9: BPK
10: RIOD
11: AFS
pp. 16-17:
1: AFS
2: RIOD
3: RIOD
4: BA
5: AFF/AFS
pp. 18-19:
6: BA
7: AKG
8: GBW
9: RIOD
10: RIOD
pp. 20-21:
1: PC
2: CS
pp. 22-23:
1: AFF/AFS
2: PC
3: GA
4: AFF/AFS
5: AFF/AFS
6: AFF/AFS
pp. 24-25:
7: BPK
8: RIOD

9: AKG
10: RIOD
11: RIOD
pp. 26-27
1: PC
2: PC
3: BAP
4: AFF/AFS
5: AFF/AFS
6: AFF/AFS
pp. 28-29:
7: RIOD
8: RIOD
9: PC
10: WL
11: GBW
pp. 30-31:
1: SF
2: AFF/AFS
3: BPK
4: AFS
5: PC
6: AFS
pp. 32-33:
7: STA
8: BPK
9: BPK
10: RIOD
11: FT
pp. 34-35:
1: PC
2: AFS
pp. 36-37:
1: AFF/AFS
2: RIOD
3: RIOD
4: AFF/AFS
5: AFF/AFS
6: AFF/AFS
pp. 38-39:
7: BPK
8: BPK
9: SF
10: SF
11: RIOD
pp. 40-41:
1: AFF/AFS
2: AFS
3: RIOD
4: AFF/AFS
5: PC
6: MA
pp. 42-43:
7: RIOD
8: BPK
9: BPK

10: RIOD
11: BPK
pp. 44-45:
1: AFF/AFS
2: RIOD
3: AFF/AFS
4: GBW
5: RIOD
pp. 46-47:
6: RIOD
7: BPK
8: RIOD
9: BPK
10: GBW
pp. 48-49:
1: CS
2: PC
pp. 50-51:
1: KLM
2: MA
3: AFS
4: AFS
pp. 52-53:
5-12: AFF/AFS
13-16: PC
17: AFS
pp. 54-55:
18: MA
19: AB
20: MA
pp. 56-57:
21: AFS
22: MA
23: AFF/AFS
pp. 58-59:
24: MA
25: RK
pp. 60-61:
26: RIOD
27: RIOD
pp. 62-63:
1: AFF/AFS
2: GB
pp. 64-65:
1: CS
2: PC
pp. 66-67:
3: RIOD
4: RIOD
5: RIOD
6: RIOD
7: RIOD
pp. 68-69:
1: CS
pp. 70-71
2: GBW
3: GBW

4: DSR
5: RIOD
6: YV
pp. 72-73:
1: CS
2: PC
pp. 74-75:
3: USHMM
4: GBW
5: GBW
6: GBW
7: BPK
pp. 76-77:
1: PC
2: AFS
3: MA
pp. 78-79:
4: GBW
5: GBW
6: RIOD
pp. 80-81:
1: NFA
2: PC
3: AFS/AFF
4: AFS
5: PC
6: AFS
pp. 82-83:
7: SE
8: GBW
9: GBW
10: PL
11: DHMB
pp. 84-85:
1: AFS
2: AFS
3: AFS
4: MA
5: AFS
6: EVZ
pp. 86-87:
7: ANP
8: PC
9: ANP
10: JEF
11: KC
pp. 88-89:
1: HNP
2: LH
3: AFS
4: JED
pp. 90-91:
5: ANP
6: TW
7: ANP
8: ANP

List of Abbreviations

AB	Allard Bovenberg, Amsterdam
AFF/AFS	Anne Frank Fonds, Basel/Anne Frank Stichting, Amsterdam
AKG	Archiv für Kunst und Geschichte, Berlin
ANP	ANP-foto, Amsterdam
BA	Bundesarchiv, Koblenz
BAP	Bildarchiv Abraham Pisarek, Berlin
BPK	Bildarchiv Preußischer Kultur besitz, Berlin
CS	Caroline Schröder, Breda
DHMB	Deutsches Historisches Museum Berlin/Photo: Gerhard Gronefeld
DSR	Dokumentations- und Kultur zentrum Deutscher Sinti und Roma, Heidelberg
EVZ	Egbert van Zon, Amsterdam
FT	Fototeca - Gabinete de Apoio à Imprensa da P.C.M., Lisbon
GA	Gemeentearchief Amsterdam
GB	Gon Buurman, Amsterdam
GBW	Galerie Bilderwelt, Reinhard Schultz, Berlin
HNP	Harry Naef Pressebilder, Zürich
IS	Institut für Stadtgeschichte, Frankfurt am Main
JED	Jan-Erik Dubbelman, Amsterdam
JEF	Jürgen Escher Fotografie, Herford
KC	Kluger Collection, Israeli Govern ment Press Office, Jerusalem
KLM	KLM Aerocarto, Arnhem
LBB	Landesbildstelle, Berlin
LH	Linda Hirsch
MA	Maria Austria Instituut, Amsterdam
NFA	Nederlands Fotoarchief, Rotterdam/Photo: Cas Oorthuys
PC	Private collection
PL	Prentenkabinet der Rijksuniversiteit Leiden/Photo: Emmy Andriesse
RIOD	Rijksinstituut voor Oorlogsdocumentatie, Amsterdam (Netherlands State Institute for War Documentation)
RK	Rode Kruis (Red Cross), The Hague
SE	Streekarchief Regio Eindhoven
SF	Spaarnestad Fotoarchief, Haarlem
STA	Stadtarchiv Aachen
TW	Transworld, Haarlem/Photo: Christopher Morris/Black Star
USHMM	United States Holocaust Memorial Museum, Washington, D.C.
WL	Wiener Library, London
YV	Yad Vashem, Jerusalem

Sources of quotations

The quotations from Anne Frank are taken from:
Frank, Anne, The Diary of a Young Girl: The Definitive Edition, edited by Otto H. Frank and Mirjam Pressler, Doubleday, New York, 1995.
p. 6: 6-20-42 / p. 8: 6-20-42 / p. 22: 6-20-42 / p. 30: 6-20-42 / p. 36: 6-20-42 / p. 40: 6-20-42 / p. 41: 6-20-42 / p. 45: 6-12-42; 7-8-42 / p. 51: 7-11-42 / p. 53: 7-11-42 / p. 54: 9-28-42, 11-19-42 / p. 55: 7-11-43, 4-6-44 / p. 57: 7-11-42, 10-9-42, 7-15-44, 3-16-44 / p. 58: 5-3-44, 6-6-44 / p. 80: 5-11-44.
Two quotations are taken from:
The Diary of Anne Frank: The Critical Edition, the Netherlands State Institute for War Documentation, Doubleday, New York, 1989. p.37: 9-28-42 / p. 44: 7-8-42
All texts by Anne Frank © Anne Frank Fonds, Basel.

7   Levi, Primo, De verdronken en de geredden, p. 52, Meulenhoff, Amsterdam 1986.

7   Frisch, Irene, "If Anne Frank had survived...," in: The Jewish Standard, 4-21-95.

7   Kennedy, John F., "Kennedy, Praising Anne Frank, Warns of New Nazi-Like Peril," in: The New York Times, 9-20-61.

7   Havel, Vaclav, at the opening of the international exhibition "Anne Frank in the World" in Prague, Czech Republic, 6-14-94.

7   Nussbaum, Laureen, "Anne Frank, schrijfster," in: De Groene Amsterdammer, 8-23-95.

7   Lev, Yehuda, "Revisiting Our Annexes," in: The Jewish Journal of Los Angeles, 3-31-95.

7   Mandela, Nelson, at the opening of the international exhibition "Anne Frank in the World" in Johannesburg, South Africa, 8-15-94.

12   Schnabel, Ernst, "Anne Frank, spur eines Kindes," p. 16, Fischer Taschenbuch Verlag, Frankfurt am Main, 1958.

16   Wilson, Cara, "The Legacy of Anne Frank," p. 50, Andrews and McMeel, Kansas City, 1995.

26   Steen, Dr. Jürgen, Wolf von Wolzogen, "Anne aus Frankfurt," p. 102, Historisches Museum, Frankfurt am Main, 1994.

38   Hofer, Walther: Der Nationalsozialismus. Dokumente 1933-1945, p. 113, Fischer Taschenbuch Verlag, Frankfurt am Main, 1957.

42   Scholl, Inge, De witte roos, p. 87, In den Toren, Baarn, 1984.

48   Miep Gies with Alison Leslie Gold, "Anne Frank Remembered," pp. 11 & 88, Simon & Schuster, New York 1987.

62   Lindwer, Willy, "De laatste zeven maanden," pp. 91, 117, 118, Gooi en Sticht, Hilversum 1988.

76   Frank, Otto, "Anne Franks Vater: Ich will Versöhnung" in: Welt am Sonntag, 2-4-79.

78   Berenbaum, Michael, "The World Must Know," p. 157, Little, Brown and Company, Boston, Toronto, London 1993.

79   Herzberg, Abel, "Schurkenrol in tragedie niet voor leiders Joodse Raad," Nieuw Israëlitisch Weekblad, 12-17-76.

84   Frank, Otto, "To all connected to the play," letter from Otto Frank, October 1955, Anne Frank Stichting archives.

88   Anne Frank 1929-1979, p. 63, Keesing Boeken bv, Amsterdam/Antwerpen 1979.

89   Mandela, Nelson, at the opening of the international exhibition "Anne Frank in the World" in Johannesburg, South Africa, 8-15-94.

91   "Herzog warnt für Verdrangen und Vergessen," in: Süddeutsche Zeitung, 4-28-95.

Colophon

ISBN 90-72972-35-x

Editing
Menno Metselaar
Ruud van der Rol
(Anne Frank House)
Final editing
Erik Somers
Also helping with this publication
Nico de Bruijn
Anneke Boekhoudt
Joséphine de Man
Mieke Sobering
(Anne Frank House)
Design
Karel Oosting
Translation
Nancy Forest-Flier
Corrections
Lorraine T. Miller, Mirjam Gerretzen
Lithography
Slothouwer Produkties, Amsterdam
Printing
De Volharding, Amsterdam
With thanks to
René Kok (RIOD)
Lutz van Dijk
Dienke Hondius
Dineke Stam
Jaap Tanja
(Supervisory group)
Jan-Erik Dubbelman
Arne Gillert
Yt Stoker
(all from the Anne Frank House)

Published and produced by the Anne Frank House

This publication was made possible in part by a contribution from the European Union.